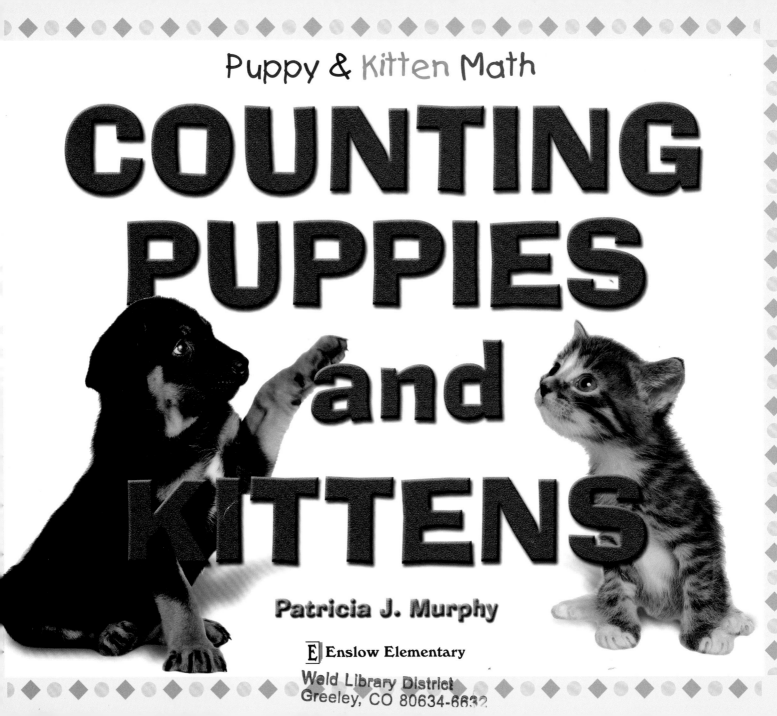

Puppy & Kitten Math

COUNTING
PUPPIES
and
KITTENS

Patricia J. Murphy

E Enslow Elementary

Contents

Words to Know

backward—To go back, in the opposite way or direction.

count—To say or think numbers in a special order. For example, 1, 2, 3 . . .

number—A word (such as *one* or *two*) or symbol (such as 1 or 2) used for counting.

tally—To keep a count, record, or score with lines called tally marks ($\cancel{||||}$).

3

Everybody Counts

Counting is thinking, saying, or writing numbers in order. You count to find HOW MANY you may have of something. Counting helps you learn about numbers.

I wish we could count!

Counting Tip: You can use your finger to point at the things you count. This will help you keep your count.

Counting from One to Ten

Counting by ones is as easy as 1–2–3. Just start with 1 and keep going. Try counting puppies and kittens up to 10.

One kitten sits on a stool.

One is the word for number 1.	We write **one** this way:	We tally **one** this way:
1				

Two puppies find a toy.

Two is the word for number 2.

2

We write **two** this way:

2

We tally **two** this way:

||

Three kittens do tricks.

Counting Tip: You can **tally** as you count. Tallying helps you keep track of the number you have counted.

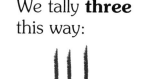

Three is the word for number 3.	We write **three** this way:	We tally **three** this way:
3	3				

Four puppies pick up sticks.

Four is the word for number 4.

4

We write **four** this way:

4

We tally **four** this way:

||||

Five puppies get a bath.

1 2 3 4 5

To tally five, draw the fifth mark across the first four.

Five is the word for number 5.

5

We write **five** this way:

5

We tally **five** this way:

卌

Six kittens play catch.

1
2
3
4
5
6

Six is the word for number 6.

6

We write **six** this way:

6

We tally **six** this way:

卌 |

Seven kittens get ready to drink milk.

1 2 3 4 5 6 7

Seven is the word for number 7.	We write **seven** this way:	We tally **seven** this way:
7	7	卌 ||

Eight puppies bark and yelp.

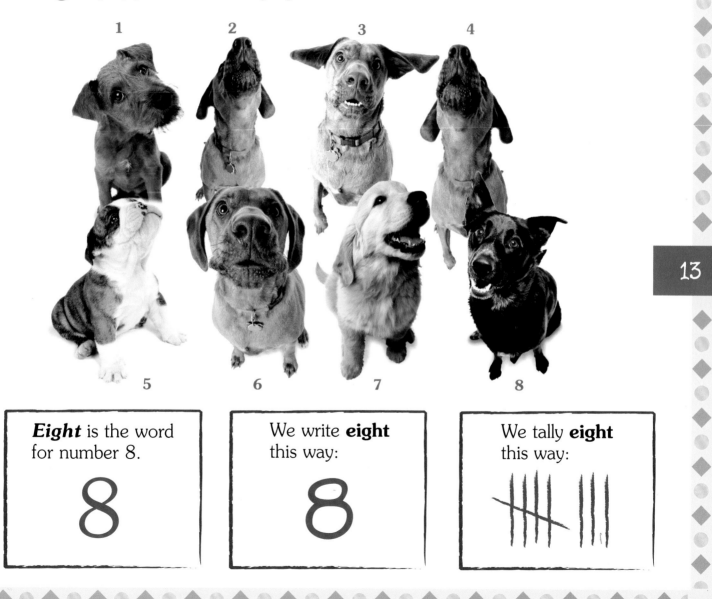

1   2   3   4

5   6   7   8

Eight is the word for number 8. 8	We write **eight** this way: 8	We tally **eight** this way: 卌 |||

Nine puppies eat treats.

Nine is the word for number 9.	We write **nine** this way:	We tally **nine** this way:
9	9										

Ten kittens fall asleep.

1 2 3 4 5

6 7 8 9 10

Counting Tip: When you make ten tally marks, draw a circle around them.

Ten is the word for number 10.

10

We write **ten** this way:

10

We tally **ten** this way:

Counting Backward from Ten

Ten sleeping kittens wake up one by one. Count the sleeping kittens before they wake up. Start at 10 and count *back* to 1.

10, 9, 8, 7, 6, 5, 4, 3, 2, 1

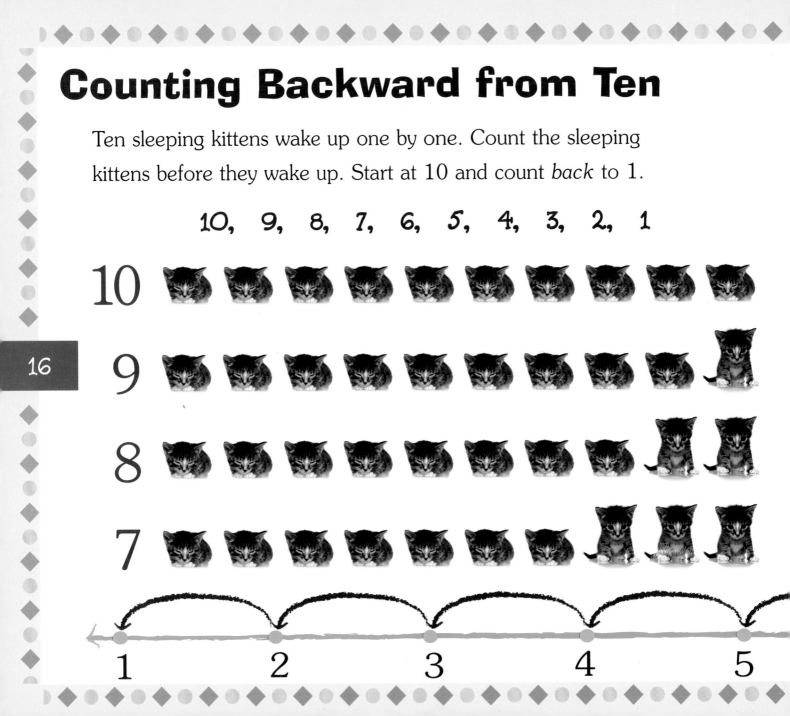

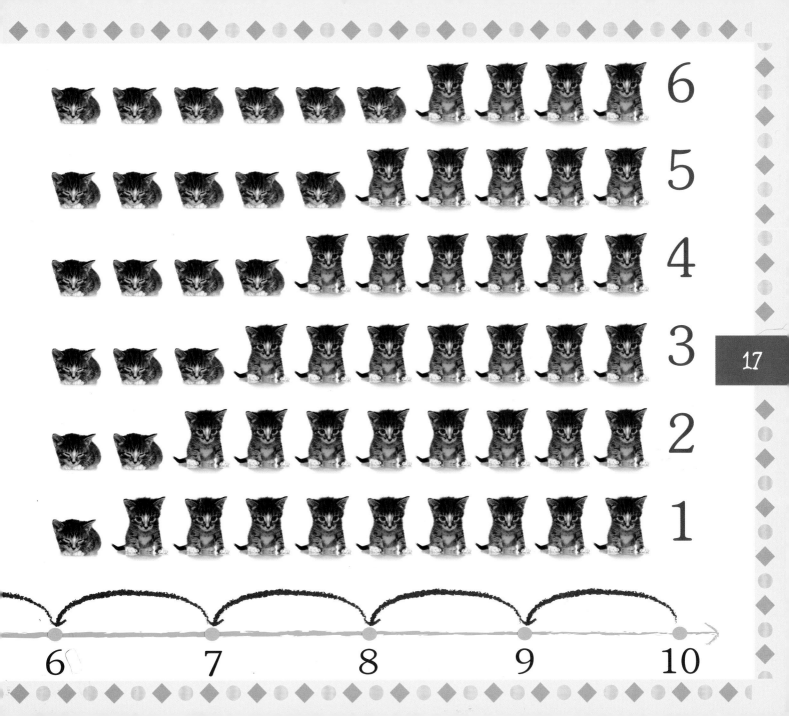

6

5

4

3

2

1

17

6   7   8   9   10

Learning About Ten and Twenty

Ten is a special number. It has a "1" and a "0." This means it has 1 group of ten and 0 ones left over.

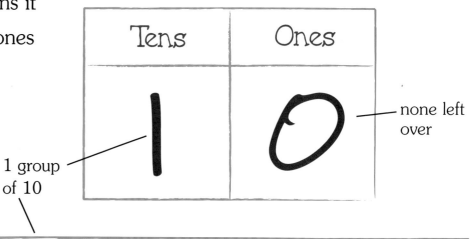

Tens	Ones
1	0

none left over

1 group of 10

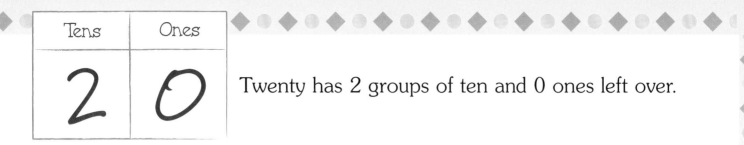

Tens	Ones
2	0

Twenty has 2 groups of ten and 0 ones left over.

Let's count to twenty!

1, 2, 3, 4, 5, 6, 7, 8, 9, 10, 11, 12, 13, 14, 15, 16, 17, 18, 19, 20

Counting by Twos

Puppies and kittens each have two ears.
Try counting their ears by twos.

To count by **twos**, count **two** at a time.
It is **two** times faster than counting by ones.

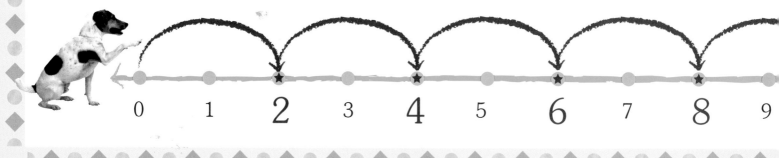

2, 4, 6, 8, 10, 12, 14, 16, 18, 20 . . .

11 **12**

13 **14** 15 **16**

17 **18**

19 **20**

21

Counting Tip: Always count two times to make sure your count is right.

10 11 12 13 14 15 16 17 18 19 20

Counting by Fives

Some puppies have lots of spots.

Try counting some spots by fives.

To count by **fives**, count **five** at a time. It is even faster than counting by twos or ones.

0 1 2 3 4 5 6 7 8 9 10 11 12 13 14 15 16 17 18 19 20 21 22

5, 10, 15, 20, 25, 30, 35, 40, 45, 50. . .

Counting Tip: You might count by fives when there is a BIG number of things to count.

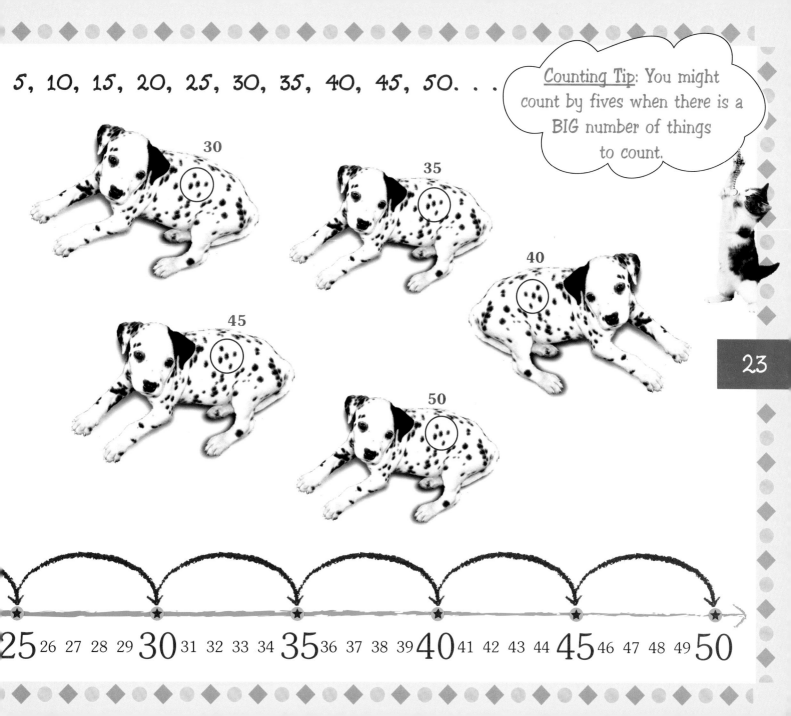

30

35

40

45

50

25 26 27 28 29 30 31 32 33 34 35 36 37 38 39 40 41 42 43 44 45 46 47 48 49 50

Counting by Tens

Puppies and kittens need to play! Count these toys by tens.

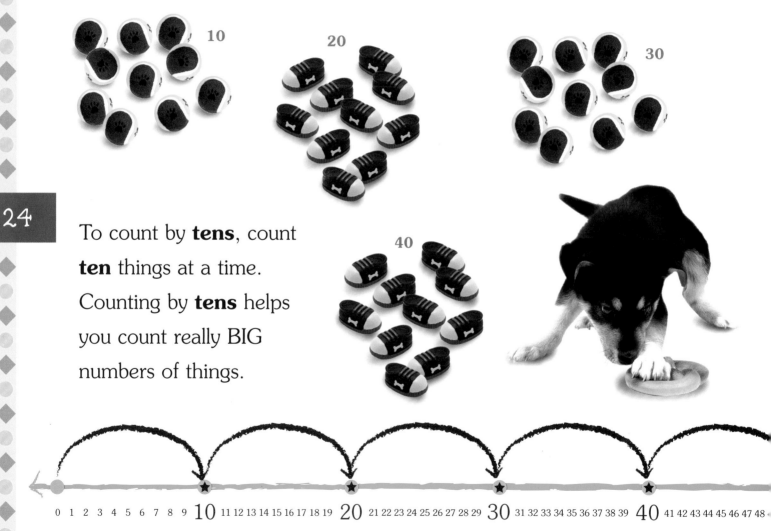

10

20

30

To count by **tens**, count **ten** things at a time. Counting by **tens** helps you count really BIG numbers of things.

40

0 1 2 3 4 5 6 7 8 9 10 11 12 13 14 15 16 17 18 19 20 21 22 23 24 25 26 27 28 29 30 31 32 33 34 35 36 37 38 39 40 41 42 43 44 45 46 47 48

10, 20, 30, 40, 50, 60, 70, 80, 90, 100 . . .

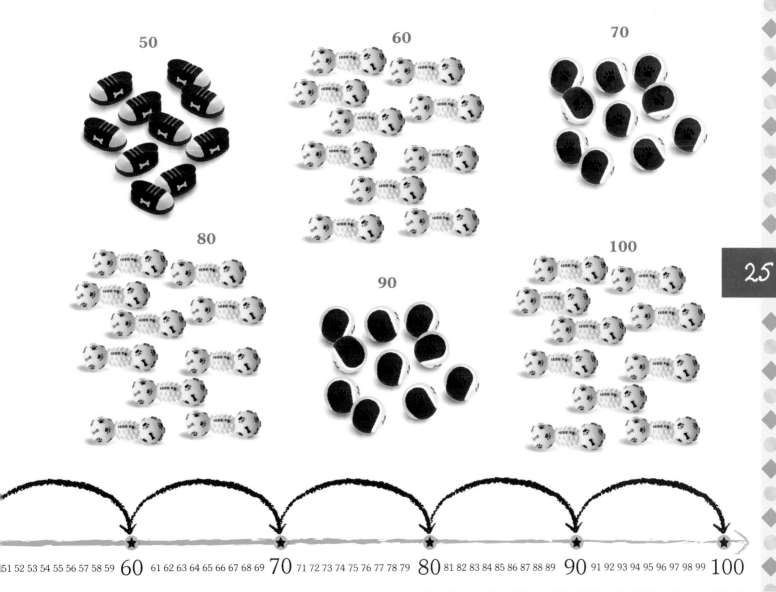

50

60

70

80

90

100

51 52 53 54 55 56 57 58 59 **60** 61 62 63 64 65 66 67 68 69 **70** 71 72 73 74 75 76 77 78 79 **80** 81 82 83 84 85 86 87 88 89 **90** 91 92 93 94 95 96 97 98 99 **100**

Counting by 25s

Small puppies and kittens can make a BIG mess.
Count their paw prints by 25s.

25

To count by **25s**, count **25** at a time.
Counting by **25s** can help you count really, really BIG numbers.

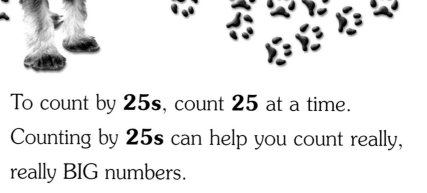

0 1 2 3 4 5 6 7 8 9 10 11 12 13 14 15 16 17 18 19 20 21 22 23 24 **25** 26 27 28 29 30 31 32 33 34 35 36 37 38 39 40 41 42 43 44 45 46 47 48

25, 50, 75, 100 . . .

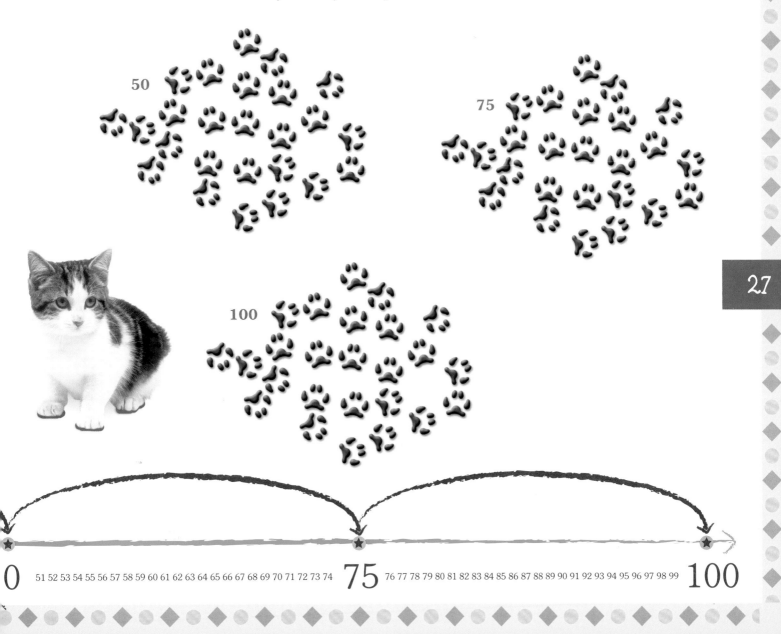

50

75

100

0   51 52 53 54 55 56 57 58 59 60 61 62 63 64 65 66 67 68 69 70 71 72 73 74   **75**   76 77 78 79 80 81 82 83 84 85 86 87 88 89 90 91 92 93 94 95 96 97 98 99   **100**

Looking Back

You can count in many different ways.

You can count by ones:

1, 2, 3, 4, 5, 6, 7, 8, 9, 10 . . .

You can count back from ten to one:

10, 9, 8, 7, 6, 5, 4, 3, 2, 1

You can count by twos: 2 – 4 – 6 – 8 – 10 – 12 – 14 – 16 – 18 – 20 . . .

You can count by fives:
5–10–15–20–25–30–35–40–45–50 . . .

You can count by tens:
10–20–30–40–50–60–70–80–90–100 . . .

You can count by 25s: 25–50–75–100 . . .

Ways to Keep Counting

Make a Counting Book
Draw pictures of puppies and kittens. Then count them and write the numbers of puppies and kittens you have on each page. Staple the pages together. Share your book with a friend.

Keep a Puppy and Kitten Watch
Take a notebook and pencil with you wherever you go. Tally the number of puppies, kittens, dogs, and cats you see along the way.

Shake on It
Have an adult help you make puppy or kitten paw prints on paper (with paint, powder, or mud). Let the paw prints dry. Count the number of paw prints and write the number on the paper. Hang your paw print picture in a special place.

Count Them All!
Count the puppies and kittens in the book by ones, twos, fives, tens, and 25s.

Tally, Tally, Tally
For a real challange, tally the total number of puppies and kittens in this book. (Start on page 1.) If you need help, just ask someone. Counting with someone is fun!*

*See page 32 for the exact total and tally.

Learn More

Books

Cameron, C.C. *One for Me, One for You*. Brookfield, Conn.: Roaring Brook Press, 2003.

Dahl, Michael. *Footprints in the Snow: Counting by Twos*. Minneapolis, Minn.: Picture Window Books, 2005.

Dahl, Michael. *Hands Down: Counting by Fives*. Minneapolis: Minn.: Picture Window Books, 2005.

Dobson, Christina. *Pizza Counting*. Watertown, Mass.: Charlesbridge, 2003.

Fisher, Valorie. *How High Can a Dinosaur Count? and Other Math Mysteries*. New York: Schwartz & Wade, 2006.

Murphy, Stuart J. *Jack the Builder*. New York: Harper Collins, 2006.

———. *Mall Mania*. New York: Harper Collins, 2006.

———. *100 Days of Cool*. New York: Harper Collins, 2004.

Thompson, Lauren. *Little Quack's Hide and Seek*. New York: Simon & Schuster Books for Young Readers, 2004.

Scherer, Jeffrey. *The Ants Go Marching*. New York: Scholastic, 2002.

Web Sites

AAA Math
<http://www.aaamath.com>

Cool Math
<http://www.coolmath.com>

Fun Brain
<http://www.funbrain.com>

Go Kidding: Math
<http://www.gokidding.com>

31

Index

Series Math Consultant
Eileen Fernández, Ph.D.
Associate Professor, Mathematics Education
Montclair State University
Montclair, NJ

Series Literacy Consultant
Allan A. De Fina, Ph.D.
Past President of the New Jersey Reading Association
Professor, Department of Literacy Education
New Jersey City University
Jersey City, NJ

To all the dogs I've ever loved

Acknowledgments: The author thanks Arlington Heights School District #25, in Arlington Heights, IL, and Lake Forest School District #67, in Lake Forest, IL, for their assistance in the research of this book.

Enslow Elementary, an imprint of Enslow Publishers, Inc.
Enslow Elementary® is a registered trademark of Enslow Publishers, Inc.

Library of Congress Cataloging-in-Publication Data

Murphy, Patricia J., 1963–
    Counting puppies and kittens / by Patricia J. Murphy.
        p. cm. — (Puppy and kitten math)
    Includes bibliographical references and index.
    ISBN-13: 978-0-7660-2724-4
    ISBN-10: 0-7660-2724-4
    1. Counting—Juvenile literature. 2. Arithmetic—Juvenile literature. I. Title.
    QA113.M883 2006
    513.2'11—dc22   2006004831

Printed in the United States of America

10 9 8 7 6 5 4 3 2 1

* There are 276 puppies and kittens in this book!

To Our Readers: We have done our best to make sure all Internet Addresses in this book were active and appropriate when we went to press. However, the author and the publisher have no control over and assume no liability for the material available on those Internet sites or on other Web sites they may link to. Any comments or suggestions can be sent by e-mail to comments@enslow.com or to the address on the back cover.

Photo credits: © 2004 Brand X Pictures, p. 20 (14, 16); Carolyn A. McKeone/Photo Researchers, Inc., p. 12 (kittens); Enslow Publishers, pp. 26–27 (paw prints); © 1999 EyeWire, Inc., p. 14 (puppies); Hemera Technologies, pp. 3, 6 (B), 10 (3), 12 (milk), 13 (1, 7, 8), 18, 19 (4, 6, 7, 8, 10, 11, 13, 14, 15, 17), 20 (2, 4, 6, 8, B), 21 (12, 18, 20), 23 (kitten), 25 (puppy), 26 (T, B, bucket), 27 (kitten); © iStockphoto.com/Gary Caviness, p. 20 (10); © iStockphoto.com/Justin Horrocks, pp. 13 (6), 28 (T); © iStockphoto.com/Mark Hayes, p. 8 (1, 2, 3); © 2006 Jupiter Images Corporation, p. 26 (M); Shutterstock, pp. 1, 2, 6 (1), 7, 8 (R), 9, 10 (1, 2, 4, 5, bucket), 11 (3, 5, 6, yarn), 12 (bowl), 13 (2, 3, 4, 5), 14 (bones), 15 (kittens), 16, 17, 19 (5, 9, 12, 16), 22, 23 (puppies), 24 (10, 20, 30, 40, 50), 25; © Warren Photographics, pp. 4–5, 11 (1, 2, 4), 19 (1, 2, 3, 18, 19, 20).

Cover photo: © Warren Photographic

Enslow Elementary
an imprint of
Enslow Publishers, Inc.
40 Industrial Road
Box 398
Berkeley Heights, NJ 07922
USA
http://www.enslow.com